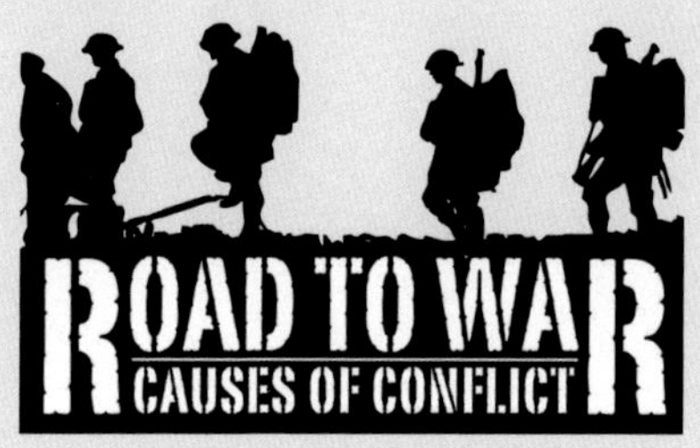

CAUSES OF THE IRAQ WAR

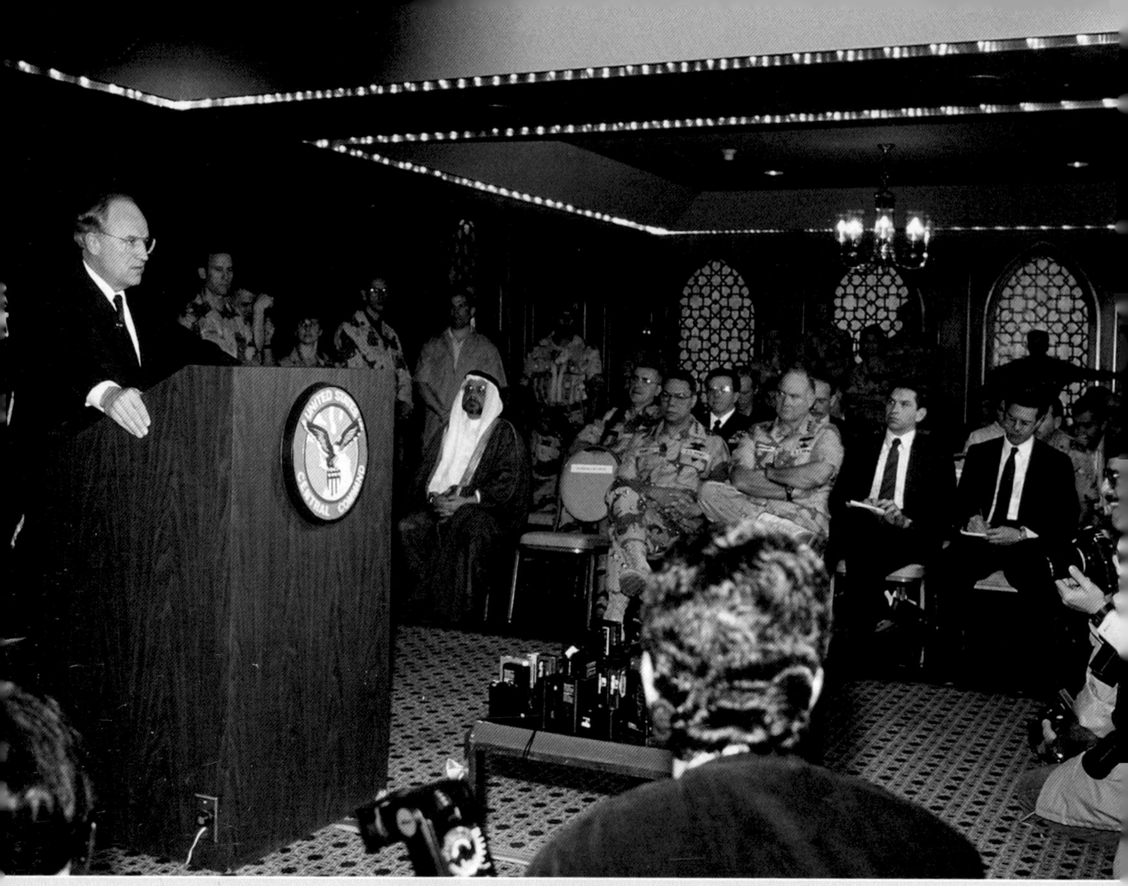

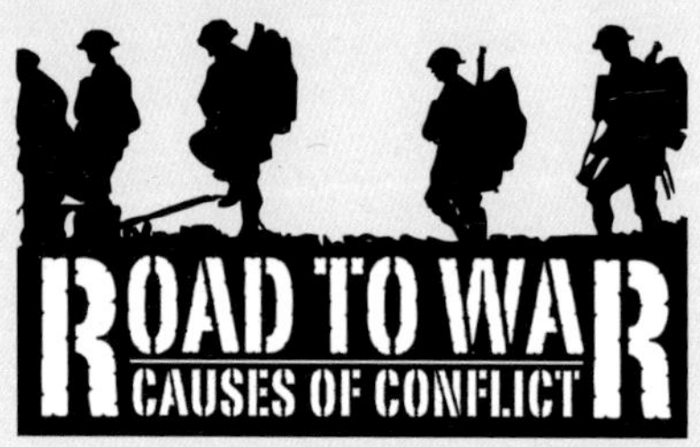

Causes of the American Revolution

Causes of the Civil War

Causes of World War I

Causes of World War II

Causes of the Iraq War

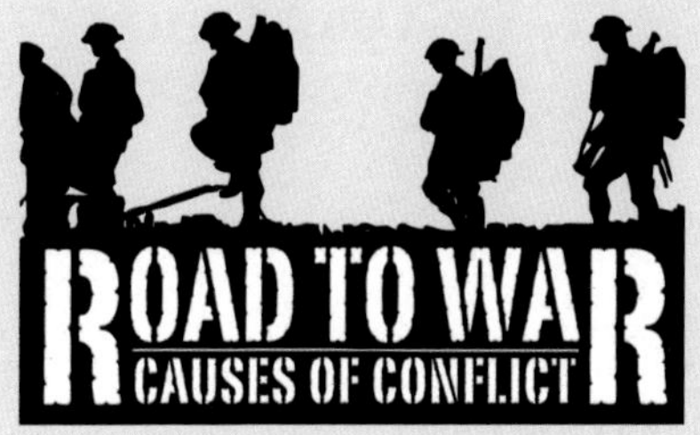

Causes of the Iraq War

Jim Gallagher

Dedication

To my son, Donald.

OTTN Publishing
16 Risler Street
Stockton, NJ 08859
www.ottnpublishing.com

Printed and bound in the United States of America.

First printing

1 3 5 7 9 8 6 4 2

Library of Congress Cataloging-in-Publication Data

Gallagher, Jim, 1969-
Causes of the Iraq war / Jim Gallagher.
p. cm. — (The road to war: causes of conflict)
Summary: "Discusses the causes of the 2003 Iraq war, explaining the origins of Iraq, the reasons for its 1990 invasion of Kuwait, the 1991 Gulf War and subsequent U.N. efforts to disarm Iraq, and the U.S. desire to remove Saddam Hussein from power"—Provided by publisher.
Includes bibliographical references and index.
ISBN-13: 978-1-59556-009-4 (hardcover)
ISBN-10: 1-59556-009-2 (hardcover)
ISBN-13: 978-1-59556-010-0 (pbk.)
ISBN-10: 1-59556-010-6 (pbk.)
1. Iraq War, 2003—Causes. I. Title. II. Series.
DS79.76.G34 2005
956.7044'31—dc22

2005015104

Frontispiece: Dick Cheney, the U.S. secretary of defense, briefs Colin Powell and Paul Wolfowitz, among others, during the 1991 Gulf War. All three would play important roles in the events leading up to the March 2003 Iraq War.

Table of Contents

Notable Figures

Tony Blair (1953–). As Great Britain's prime minister, Blair supported a December 1998 strike against Iraq and was George W. Bush's strongest ally during the months leading up to the 2003 invasion.

George H. W. Bush (1924–). The 41st president of the United States, Bush built a political and military coalition opposed to Saddam Hussein and launched the 1991 Gulf War.

George W. Bush (1946–). Although he initially followed a policy of containing Iraq through U.N. sanctions, after the September 11, 2001, terrorist attacks the 43rd president embraced the policy of preemptive war and planned to force Saddam Hussein from power.

Dick Cheney (1941–). As secretary of defense, Cheney directed U.S. military activity during the 1991 Gulf War. Elected vice president in 2000, he helped develop the Bush administration policies that would be used to justify the 2003 invasion of Iraq.

Bill Clinton (1946–). President Clinton believed that Iraq possessed weapons of mass destruction. When Saddam Hussein refused to cooperate with U.N. inspectors in 1998, Clinton ordered Operation Desert Fox, a three-day bombing campaign.

Saddam Hussein (1937–). As president of Iraq from 1979 to 2003, Saddam Hussein started wars against Iran (1980) and Kuwait (1990). He also used his military to repress Iraq's civilian population, killing hundreds of thousands of people. His efforts to acquire weapons of

Dick Cheney

Donald Rumsfeld

Paul Wolfowitz

mass destruction led to repeated condemnation by the United Nations.

Jabir al-Ahmad al-Jabir al-Sabah (1926–). The emir of Kuwait asked for U.S. help after his country was invaded by Iraq in 1990. In 2003, Kuwait was one of the few Arab countries that publicly supported the invasion of Iraq.

Hosni Mubarak (1928–). As president of Egypt, the largest Arab country, Mubarak attempted to mediate the 1990 Iraq-Kuwait crisis. In 1991, Mubarak sent Egyptian troops to help liberate Kuwait; however, he publicly opposed the 2003 invasion of Iraq.

Colin Powell (1937–). During the 1990–91 Gulf crisis, Powell was President George H. W. Bush's top military adviser. In 2002, as secretary of state, Powell encouraged the United Nations to support regime change in Iraq.

Donald Rumsfeld (1932–). Secretary of Defense Rumsfeld was an advocate of both preemptive war and the use of U.S. force to protect American interests around the world. He led the planning for the 2003 invasion of Iraq.

Paul Wolfowitz (1943–). A longtime advocate of removing Saddam Hussein from power, Deputy Secretary of Defense Wolfowitz helped formulate the Bush Doctrine, arguing that preemptive war could be justified as self-defense.

SEAL OF THE PRESIDENT OF THE UNITED STATES

During a nationally televised speech on March 17, 2003, President George W. Bush claimed that diplomacy had failed to force Iraq to disarm. "All the decades of deceit and cruelty have now reached an end," Bush declared. "Saddam Hussein and his sons must leave Iraq within 48 hours. Their refusal to do so will result in military conflict, commenced at a time of our choosing."

1

A Deadline for War

There was little activity in Baghdad during the predawn hours of March 20, 2003. Most residents of Iraq's capital city were sleeping. A handful of early risers driving to their jobs shared the nearly deserted highways, while in the neighborhood markets known as *souqs*, shopkeepers prepared to open their stores for another day of business.

Unlike the sleepy civilian areas, air-defense stations around Baghdad bustled with activity. Technicians anxiously peered at radar screens, while crews manned anti-aircraft guns. Iraq's military was on high alert, expecting an attack at any moment. Two days earlier, the president of the United States had given Iraq's dictator, Saddam Hussein, 48 hours to leave the country. In a speech broadcast around the world, President George W. Bush threatened that if Saddam refused to step down, the United States and its allies would invade Iraq. Now that deadline had come and gone, with Saddam still in Baghdad.

The dictator's defiance was not surprising. For more than 20 years, Saddam Hussein had disregarded world opinion. During his rule, Saddam started wars against his neighbors Iran and Kuwait. He actively worked to develop ***weapons of mass destruction*** (WMD)—nuclear, chemical, and biological weapons capable of killing large numbers of people. He had violated international treaties by using these deadly weapons. Over the years, his regime had brutally murdered hundreds of thousands of Iraqi citizens to maintain power. For these reasons, Saddam had long been considered one of the world's most dangerous men.

After Iraq invaded and occupied Kuwait in August 1990, the international community rallied to oppose the dictator's plans to dominate the Middle East. An alliance of nations, led by the United States, worked together through the United Nations (U.N.) to oust Saddam's forces from Kuwait. When this brief conflict, known as the 1991 Gulf War, ended, the U.N. set conditions for peace. The Security Council, a powerful branch of the organization responsible for maintaining world peace and security, outlined Iraq's obligations in a series of ***resolutions***. These required Iraq to give up its weapons of mass destruction. A special group, the United Nations Special Commission (UNSCOM), was created to make sure that Iraq actually disarmed.

But even though Saddam agreed to abide by the U.N. resolutions, his government tried to interfere with the UNSCOM inspections. This led to several confrontations between the United States and Iraq during the 1990s.

In November 2002, the U.N. Security Council passed Resolution 1441, which gave Iraq a "final opportunity" to disarm. Facing the threat of war, Saddam agreed to comply. However, when initial reports indicated that Iraq still was not cooperating with inspectors, Bush declared that Saddam's time had run out. Despite bitter opposition in the United Nations, the United States and its allies prepared for war.

The suspense did not last long for the Iraqi soldiers on duty in Baghdad on the morning of March 20. At about 5:30 A.M.—some 90 minutes after Bush's deadline had passed—a series of explosions rocked the capital. People in southern Baghdad were awakened by the sound of air-raid sirens, as bombs and jet-propelled cruise missiles slammed into buildings. The Iraq War had begun.

Mesopotamia, as Iraq was once known, contains many monuments to the ancient civilizations that flourished there. The tower of this ninth-century Muslim mosque in Samarra rises to a height of 171 feet (52 meters).

2

Colonialism, Nationalism, and Oil

The 2003 Iraq War—and the Gulf War, fought a dozen years earlier—occurred for many complex reasons. The root causes of these two conflicts can be traced back to events that took place long before the country of Iraq even existed. Modern Iraq includes the area between the Tigris and Euphrates Rivers, known in ancient times as Mesopotamia, where one of the world's first civilizations flourished some 5,500 years ago.

Over the centuries, different empires ruled Mesopotamia. Around the year 1534, the Ottoman Empire took control of Mesopotamia. This mighty empire stretched across northern Africa, the Middle East, eastern Europe, and western Asia.

The Ottoman sultans were Muslims, but their widespread empire contained people of many different races and cultures. To rule effectively, the sultans created a network of local governments. Mesopotamia was divided into three *vilayets*, or provinces. The mountainous territory in the north was ruled from the city of Mosul. A central province was ruled from Baghdad. The southern province was ruled from the city of Basra. The Ottoman sultans appointed *pashas*, or governors, to rule over each *vilayet* and sent soldiers to enforce their laws.

The Ottoman rulers also claimed the nearby Arabian Peninsula, but it was mostly uninhabited desert. Around the year 1744, though, an Arab tribe called the Bani Utub established a small settlement on the Persian Gulf coast south of Basra. In 1756, Sabah bin Jabir bin Adhabi became *emir*, or ruler, of the community, which became known as Kuwait.

Kuwait was poor and unimportant, so the Ottoman sultans allowed Sabah bin Jabir and his descendants, the al-Sabah family, to rule the land on behalf of their empire. In exchange, Kuwait's emirs were expected to pay ***tribute*** to the pasha of Basra. In reality, though, the sultans had little control over Kuwait, and the emirs rarely paid the tribute.

Ottoman armies could easily have crushed the tiny emirate. However, the sultans were struggling with more important problems. One of these was pressure from European countries like Russia, France, and Great Britain, which were competing for colonies. ***Colonialism*** allowed the European countries to build worldwide empires using the native labor and natural resources of their colonies. During the 18th and 19th centuries, the European colonial powers began to invade and conquer Ottoman territories in Africa and Europe.

At the same time, the sultans were dealing with unrest within their borders. In response to the large empires of the time, a movement called ***nationalism*** developed during the 19th century. Nationalities—groups of people who shared a history, culture, and language—began trying to break away from the imperial powers. These groups, including the Arabs in the Ottoman Empire, wanted to create independent countries. The Ottoman sultans tried to stop the spread of Arab nationalism by arresting leaders and repressing the people. Coupled with the external pressure as European powers grabbed Ottoman territories, the internal unrest weakened the empire.

In 1899, Emir Mubarak asked Britain to help Kuwait become independent from Ottoman control.

By the early 20th century, European nations like Great Britain, France, and Russia ruled colonies all over the world. These imperial powers exploited the people and natural resources of the territories they governed to strengthen and enrich their empires. However, natives of the colonies often resented being ruled by a foreign power. As a result, nationalists began to work for the creation of independent new states that would be free from European interference.

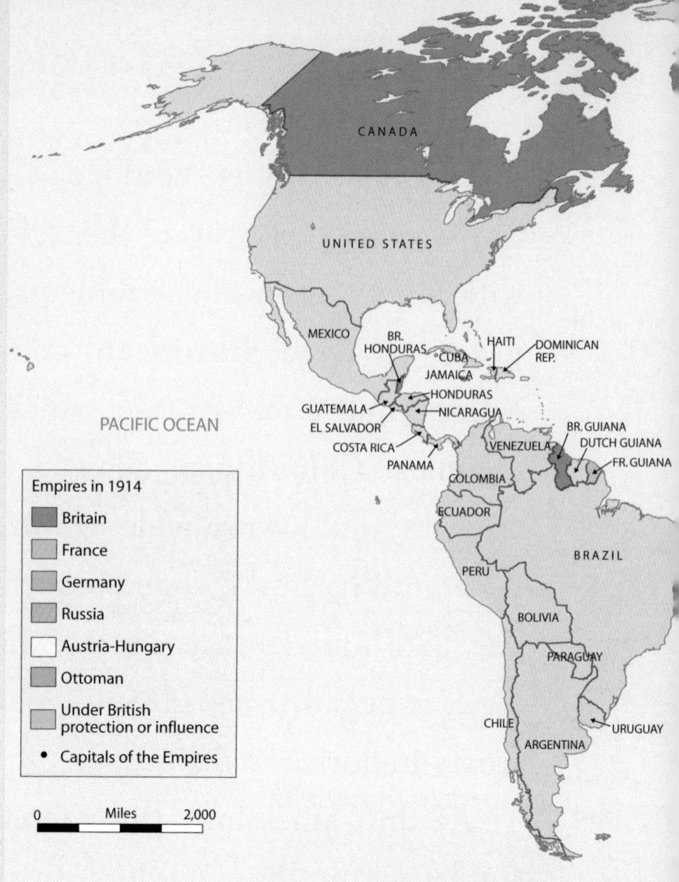

The British were interested because of Kuwait's location on the Persian Gulf. To maintain its empire, Britain needed to protect ships traveling to and from its colonies. Mubarak promised to build a naval base where British warships could stop for fuel and supplies while patrolling the waters around the empire's most important colony, India. The Ottoman rulers were angry, but there was nothing they could do. Although they continued to claim Kuwait, their empire had become too weak to challenge Britain.

The Gulf region became even more important after 1908, when oil was discovered in Persia (modern-day

Iran). Oil could be used to run machinery in factories and power the engines of trains, ships, and automobiles. Britain quickly reached an agreement to buy oil from Persia and began looking for the valuable resource in Kuwait and Mesopotamia. In 1913, the emir of Kuwait secretly promised to let Britain develop any oil fields found in his country.

To make this arrangement legal, Kuwait's murky status needed to be clarified. In 1913, British and Ottoman leaders negotiated the Anglo-Ottoman Convention. The treaty declared that Kuwait would be an ***autonomous*** part of the Ottoman Empire. This would allow the emir to sell oil to Britain. The treaty never went into effect, however. Before it could be ratified, World War I broke out in Europe in August 1914.

The Ottoman Empire entered the fighting on the side of Germany and Austria-Hungary (these became known as the Central Powers). Facing them were the Allied Powers, led by Great Britain, France, and Russia. In 1915, Britain formally declared Kuwait an independent British ***protectorate***. British soldiers from India soon invaded Mesopotamia to protect their Persian oil supply. By October 1918, when the Ottoman Empire asked for peace, Britain controlled the Ottoman territories of the Middle East.

At the end of the war, the victorious Allies broke up the Ottoman Empire, creating new nations. Arabs who had fought with the Allies wanted an independent Arab state stretching from Egypt to Mesopotamia. They felt betrayed when the British and French instead divided Arab lands into small countries. One of these was Iraq, created from the Ottoman provinces of Mosul, Baghdad, and Basra.

The Arabs grew angrier when they learned that their countries would not be fully independent. The League of Nations, an organization created after the war to prevent future conflicts through negotiation and diplomacy, established a system in which new

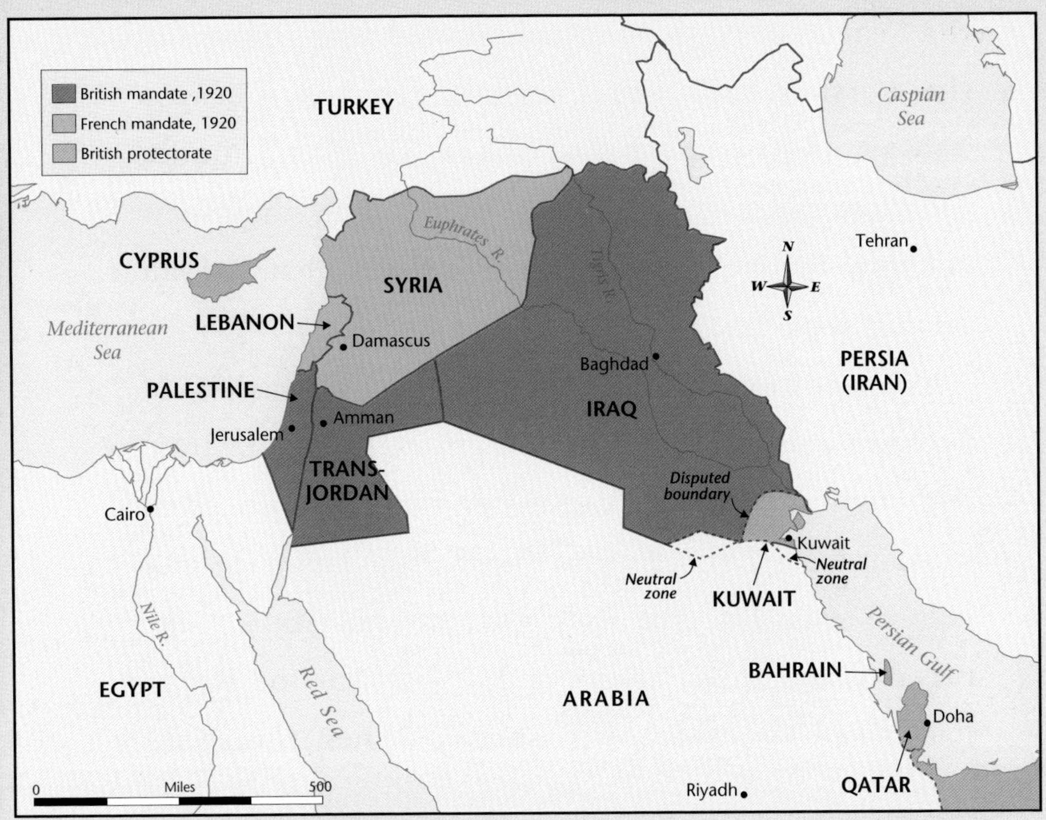

This map shows how the Middle East was divided into French and British spheres of influence after World War I. Through the mandate system, Britain gained control of the newly formed country Iraq.

countries were placed under the authority of a major power like Britain or France. The major powers were supposed to help the new countries establish good governments and social institutions. Because of Iraq's strategic location and potential oil reserves, Britain asked for the ***mandate*** to rule Iraq.

Iraqis saw the mandate system as a new form of colonialism—a way Britain could exploit their country's resources. Iraqis also resented the borders set by the League of Nations, which limited Iraq's access to the Persian Gulf. Iraqi leaders felt that because Kuwait had once been linked to Basra under Ottoman rule, it should be included in their new country. Britain, however, had insisted that Kuwait remain separate.

These problems were complicated by a history of hostility between the different ethnic groups in Iraq. Although most people were Arabs, in the north lived a group called the Kurds. The Kurds' language and culture was different from that of the Arabs. Like other nationalities, at the end of the war the Kurds had asked for their own country. When the Allies ignored their request, some Kurds prepared to fight both the British and the Arabs for independence.

Religion was also an issue. Although most Iraqis were Muslims, there are two major branches of this religion, Sunni Islam and Shia Islam. These two branches do not agree on how Islam should be practiced, and throughout history they have fought bloody religious wars. Most Arabs in Mesopotamia were followers of Shia Islam, or Shiites. However, the Ottoman sultans had been Sunni Muslims. During their rule most government officials had also been Sunnis, and Shiites had faced discrimination. When the British set up Iraq's new government, they gave the educated and experienced Sunni administrators a prominent role. This angered the Shiites.

Opposition to British rule, combined with ethnic and religious differences, caused revolts to erupt throughout Iraq in 1920. The British sent troops to put down the rebellion. However, occasional fighting occurred throughout the decade.

By the early 1930s, British leaders felt Iraq was ready for full independence. First, however, the League of Nations said that Iraq had to accept the border with Kuwait. In July 1932, Iraq's prime minister agreed to recognize the existing border, and the next month Iraq became independent.

Britain remained influential in both Iraq and Kuwait. Over the next few decades, British advisers helped develop the oil industry in both countries. But although Iraq's kings maintained friendly relations with Great Britain, many Iraqis were unhappy about British involvement in their country's affairs.

In 1948, India became independent, so during the 1950s British leaders decided they no longer needed naval bases in the Persian Gulf. But as the British were making plans to withdraw from the region, radical changes occurred in Iraq. In 1958, a group of Iraqi army officers rebelled against the pro-British government. They captured and executed the king

General Abd al-Karim Qasim made major changes to Iraq's oil industry. His government took over the companies that produced and exported oil, and played a key role in the creation of OPEC in 1960.

and other government leaders. An Iraqi general named Abd al-Karim Qasim became dictator of Iraq.

Qasim wanted Iraq to play a more important role in world affairs, without interference from foreigners. The dictator passed laws that gave Iraq's government control over the country's oil. Qasim also invited leaders from Kuwait, Iran, Saudi Arabia, and Venezuela to a meeting in Baghdad. There, they formed the Organization of Petroleum Exporting Countries (OPEC) in September 1960. A goal of OPEC was to control the international price of oil. To do this, each OPEC member agreed to a quota, or limit, on the amount of oil it would produce each year. In theory this would keep the supply of oil low, which would raise the price and ensure that OPEC members earned a significant profit.

Kuwait's oil industry was the strongest of the OPEC countries. Money from oil sales had been invested in factories and infrastructure, making Kuwait the most economically developed country in the region. The British felt Kuwait was ready to stand alone, so in June 1961 they withdrew their troops and the emir proclaimed his country's independence.

Almost immediately, Qasim declared that Kuwait rightfully belonged to Iraq. He ignored the 1932 border agreement, citing instead the 1913 Anglo-Ottoman Convention to justify his claim that Kuwait had once been part of the Basra province under Ottoman rule, and should therefore be part of Iraq. Qasim moved Iraqi troops to a threatening position on the border with Kuwait. However, facing opposition from Great Britain and the other Arab countries, Qasim backed down from his threat.

Qasim did not remain in power for long—he was assassinated two years later. After his death, Iraq's new government wanted friendly relations with Kuwait. In 1963, it signed another agreement that formally recognized the existing border.

Rising Tensions in the Gulf

An Iraqi soldier walks through a desolate landscape littered with the corpses of Iranian soldiers. The 1980–88 Iran-Iraq War was a brutal conflict that placed Iraq in a desperate financial position. Saddam Hussein (bottom left) became angry when other Arab states refused to write off Iraq's war debts.

3

By the late 1960s, an organization called the Baath Party had taken control of Iraq's government. The Arabic word *Baath* means "resurrection" or "renaissance," and the party was dedicated to promoting Arab nationalism and opposing the influence of Western countries in the Arab world. The leader of the Baath Party, Ahmad Hasan al-Bakr, became president of Iraq in 1968. His second-in-command was a man named Saddam

Hussein. Saddam used his powerful position to attack enemies of the Baath Party. Sunni Muslims were given important jobs in the government and military, while Shiites and Kurds were persecuted.

Eventually, Saddam was ready to take complete control of the party. In July 1979, he announced that his political rivals had been involved in a plot to overthrow the government. He had them arrested, tried for treason, and executed. Al-Bakr was forced to retire, and Saddam took over as president.

At around the same time, neighboring Iran was also undergoing a violent change in government. The shah, or ruler, of Iran was unpopular, in part because his government used brutal tactics to maintain order. In late 1978, a Shiite Muslim leader named Ayatollah Ruhollah Khomeini inspired nationwide protests against the shah. In January 1979, the shah left the country, never to return. Khomeini and his supporters soon established a new government in Iran based on Islamic law.

Saddam Hussein saw the unrest in Iran as both a danger and an opportunity. Iraqis had always considered Iran a potential enemy. Iran was the largest country in the Persian Gulf region, with more than twice as many citizens as Iraq. When Khomeini encouraged Shiites in other Gulf countries to rise up against their leaders, the Baath Party felt threat-

After seizing power in Iran in 1979, Ayatollah Ruhollah Khomeini encouraged Shiite Muslims to rise up against the secular Arab governments of the Persian Gulf region. This threatened Saddam's power. In response, Iraq attacked Iran in September 1980.

ened. However, Khomeini had powerful enemies, including the United States, which had supported the shah's government. After radical Iranian students seized the U.S. embassy in Tehran and took its staff hostage, U.S. leaders imposed ***economic sanctions*** that were intended to isolate Iran and weaken Khomeini's regime. Saddam saw this as a chance for Iraq to replace Iran as the major regional power. In September 1980, Iraq's army invaded Iran.

Iraq's army was well trained and supplied with modern equipment. It quickly captured 1,000 square miles of Iranian territory. However, the Iranian army regrouped and launched counteroffensives in 1981 and 1982 that recaptured most of the territory. By 1983, Iran and Iraq were at a ***stalemate***. Iraq had better equipment, but Iran had more soldiers available. Neither country could win a decisive victory.

The Iran-Iraq War was one of the most brutal wars in modern history. Both sides launched attacks against enemy civilians and against neutral ships in the Persian Gulf. Iraqi forces used deadly chemical weapons against Iranian soldiers. During the war, Saddam Hussein's military even used chemical weapons against his own citizens. Some Kurds had sided with the Iranians when they invaded northern Iraq, so when Iran was forced to withdraw, Saddam punished the rebellious Kurds. The most infamous gas attack occurred in March 1988, when more than 5,000 Kurdish civilians were killed in the village of Halabja. Dozens of other Kurdish villages in northern Iraq were also gassed or destroyed by the military.

Supplying an army during wartime is very expensive. Iraq spent $120 billion on the military between 1981 and 1985. At the same time, Iraq's oil revenues plunged from more than $26 billion a year in 1980 to less than $9 billion by 1982. To continue its war with

A Kurdish man and his child lie dead outside their home in the Iraqi village of Halabja. They were among more than 5,000 Iraqi Kurds killed in a notorious chemical gas attack in 1988 that was ordered by Saddam Hussein.

Iran, Iraq borrowed billions of dollars from Kuwait, Saudi Arabia, and other Arab countries. The United States also loaned money to Iraq.

The Iran-Iraq War ended in August 1988, when the United Nations stepped in and negotiated a cease-fire. More than 600,000 Iranians and 375,000 Iraqis had been killed during the eight-year war, and over a million people had become refugees.

Iraq was in a desperate financial position when the war ended. It owed $77 billion to other countries, and it needed another $230 billion to rebuild its devastated cities and factories. But Iraq did not have enough money to rebuild and repay its debts. Most of the government's money went toward the military. Iraq could have saved billions for reconstruction by reducing the size of the army. However, Saddam was afraid to do this. Jobs were scarce, and unhappy, out-of-work soldiers might try to overthrow his government.

One way Iraq could raise more money would be to sell more oil. But during the 1980s new sources of oil had been found, and by 1988 there was an oil ***glut***. Kuwait and the United Arab Emirates (UAE) made this problem worse by pumping more than their OPEC quotas. Because more oil was available than was needed, the price of oil had fallen sharply, from about $35 a barrel in 1982 to $15 a barrel in 1988. Iraq's oil minister estimated that for every dollar off the price of a barrel of oil, Iraq lost about a billion dollars in potential revenue each year.

At an OPEC meeting in December 1988, Iraq asked for a higher quota so it could sell more oil. It also insisted that other OPEC members stop producing more than their own quotas, so the price of oil would rise to a higher level. OPEC did agree to increase Iraq's quota slightly, but not as much as Saddam wanted. Meanwhile, Kuwait and the UAE continued to exceed their production quotas.

Iraq also sought relief from its crushing financial obligations. In February 1990, at a meeting of Arab leaders in Jordan, Saddam asked Iraq's ***creditors*** to forgive his country's debts. Iraq had prevented Iran's Shiite Islamic Revolution from spreading to Arab countries where Sunni Muslims held power, Saddam claimed, and the leaders of those countries could show their gratitude by writing off Iraq's debt. Despite this argument, Iraq's creditors still demanded their money.

Meanwhile, the rest of the world was beginning to take a hard look at Iraq. In the United States, Saddam Hussein was criticized for his repression of the Kurds and his harsh treatment of political dissidents. He was condemned for using chemical weapons during the Iran-Iraq War. Experts worried that the dictator was developing other weapons of mass destruction as well. It was common knowledge that Iraq wanted nuclear weapons. In 1981, Israeli warplanes had destroyed Iraq's Osirak nuclear reactor just before it went online. The reactor would have been able to produce fuel for a nuclear bomb. During March 1990, British customs agents arrested five men who were trying to smuggle electrical switches to Iraq. The switches could be used to trigger a nuclear weapon. In April, the British seized another illicit weapon-related shipment to Iraq. These incidents increased concerns about Iraq's WMD programs.

As international pressure mounted, Saddam became defiant. In April 1990, he declared that if Israel attacked Iraq again, he would launch chemical warheads against it. He also condemned Israel for its occupation of the West Bank and Gaza territories, which it had captured in a June 1967 war. Saddam also had harsh words for Israel's closest ally, the United States. He denounced "American imperialism,"

Despite Iraq's threats, Kuwait under Emir Jabir al-Ahmad al-Jabir al-Sabah continued to pump more than its OPEC quota in 1989 and 1990.

claiming that the United States wanted to dominate the Arabs because of their oil. Many Arabs considered the dictator a hero for standing up to the United States and Israel.

In May 1990, the Arab Leaque held a special meeting in Baghdad. The purpose of the meeting was to unite the Arab countries in condemning Israel. But during the conference, Saddam showed that he was also angry at the leaders of Gulf Arab states. He complained that the wealthy Arab states had refused to write off Iraq's debts, and he threatened military action against any OPEC country that continued to exceed its production quota.

Saddam repeated this threat privately at a July 16 OPEC meeting. He also claimed that during the Iran-Iraq War, Kuwait had stolen oil from Iraq's side of the Rumaila oil field, located on the border between the two countries.

On July 17, 1990, in a nationally televised speech, Saddam complained that Kuwait and the UAE had "stabbed Iraq in the back with a poisoned dagger." He said, "Instead of rewarding Iraq, which sacrificed the blossoms of its youth in the war to protect their houses of wealth, they are severely harming it." Saddam accused his neighbors of conspiring with the United States and Israel against Iraq, and he threatened

Although Saddam promised Hosni Mubarak (right) that he would not attack Kuwait unless diplomacy failed, Iraq's representatives withdrew from peace talks after two days.

military action. The next day, 30,000 Iraqi soldiers moved to the border with Kuwait.

Kuwait's ruler, Emir Jabir al-Ahmad al-Jabir al-Sabah, quickly asked other countries to help resolve the crisis. Egyptian president Hosni Mubarak offered to mediate the dispute. Mubarak met with Saddam Hussein on July 25, and the dictator promised that he would not attack unless the two sides were unable to resolve the crisis peacefully. The Egyptians arranged a peace conference in Saudi Arabia.

That same day, Saddam met with April Glaspie, the U.S. ambassador to Iraq. Saddam angrily presented Iraq's complaints against both Kuwait and the United States. Glaspie tried to calm him down, saying that the United States wanted a better relationship with Iraq. The ambassador was happy to learn about the peace conference. Shortly after the meeting, she told President George H. W. Bush that war could be avoided. However, Saddam may have misinterpreted some of Glaspie's comments as a sign that the United States would not intervene if Iraq attacked Kuwait.

On July 31 and August 1, emissaries from Iraq and Kuwait held talks in Saudi Arabia. However, even though Kuwait promised to stop overproducing oil and to forgive Iraq's war debts, the talks collapsed. At 2 A.M. on August 2, Iraq's army swept into Kuwait. Kuwait's small military was unable to stop the invasion. The emir and his family fled, and within a few hours Saddam Hussein controlled the country.

The World Responds

President George H. W. Bush (bottom left) took the lead in formulating the international response to Iraq's invasion. "This will not stand, this aggression against Kuwait," the U.S. leader promised on August 5, 1990. Two days later, the United States sent troops to protect Saudi Arabia.

The world reacted quickly to Iraq's aggression. Within a few hours, the U.N. Security Council had passed Resolution 660, which condemned the invasion and demanded the immediate withdrawal of all Iraqi forces from Kuwait. On August 6, the Security Council set up economic sanctions against Iraq (Resolution 661), and on August 9, it declared Iraq's seizure of Kuwait "null and void" under international law (Resolution 662).

President Bush condemned Iraq's "naked aggression" and halted U.S. trade with Iraq. He sent U.S. warships to the Gulf and spoke with key allies like Prime Minister Margaret Thatcher of Great Britain, Egypt's Hosni Mubarak, and the Soviet premier, Mikhail Gorbachev. Gradually, world leaders began to formulate a response to Saddam's actions.

Because Western economies depended on oil from the Middle East, Bush felt it was important to defend Saudi Arabia. His secretary of defense, Dick Cheney, and top military adviser, Colin Powell, were sent to warn King Fahd that an Iraqi attack might be imminent. At first the Saudis refused offers of help, but by August 7 they had changed their minds. American soldiers soon arrived in Saudi Arabia, where they quickly built defensive positions near the border.

Saddam Hussein was surprised at the reaction to his conquest. On August 12, he offered to withdraw if Israel pulled out of the occupied territories. Although this proposal appealed to some people in the Arab world, the United States and its allies refused to negotiate. The U.N. insisted that Iraq withdraw immediately. Instead, on August 28, Saddam officially declared Kuwait the 19th province of Iraq.

Using sandbags and entrenching tools, U.S. soldiers construct temporary defensive positions around an airbase in the Arabian desert, August 1990. The American deployment to protect Saudi Arabia became known as Operation Desert Shield.

On October 29, the U.N. Security Council passed Resolution 674. This said that if Iraq continued to ignore its demands to leave Kuwait, the U.N. would take "further measures"—possibly including the use of military force—to remove the Iraqi army. The resolution also called for Iraq to pay a fine for the damages it had caused.

During this time, Bush negotiated with other world leaders to build a ***coalition*** of allies. Eventually, 34 nations joined the coalition, providing soldiers or financial support to the effort. The United States would provide the largest military force—by mid-November,

Coalition tanks rumble through the Iraqi desert, February 1991.

450,000 U.S. soldiers were stationed in the Persian Gulf. Saddam reacted by sending another 400,000 soldiers to Kuwait.

On November 29, the U.N. Security Council passed Resolution 678. If Saddam refused to leave Kuwait by January 15, 1991, the allied coalition could use military force to free the emirate. The deadline passed with Iraqi forces still occupying the country. At 3 A.M. on January 17, coalition air forces attacked Baghdad. The 1991 Gulf War had begun.

Over the next five weeks, bombs and missiles destroyed strategic targets in Iraq and Kuwait, including government buildings, electrical plants, radar stations, and Scud missile launchers. With Saddam's defenses weakened, a ground assault began on February 24. U.S., British, and French tank divisions penetrated deep into Iraq, while U.S. Marines and a force made up of Egyptians, Syrians, and soldiers from other Arab countries pushed into Kuwait. Iraq's army was overmatched, and by February 27 the coalition had liberated Kuwait.

Some people wanted the coalition to continue on to Baghdad to overthrow Saddam Hussein. However, the United Nations had only authorized the coalition to free Kuwait. Also, Arab members of the coalition, such as Saudi Arabia and Egypt, opposed a full-scale invasion of Iraq. Thus, the decision was made to halt the attack. On February 28—about 100 hours after the ground war began—President Bush declared a cease-fire. But he encouraged Iraqi citizens to rise up and overthrow their oppressive dictator.

As Iraqis fled from Kuwait, they started fires in the country's oil fields, creating a major ecological disaster.

At the end of the war, coalition leaders permitted the Iraqi army to keep its weapons and helicopters. This would enable Saddam Hussein to put down revolts by his Shiite and Kurdish citizens and remain in power.

The U.N. Security Council set the conditions for peace. Resolution 686 said that Iraq had to give up its claim to Kuwait, return all property and prisoners seized during the occupation, and accept financial responsibility for the damage caused by the invasion. Resolution 687 established the border between Iraq and Kuwait and set up a demilitarized buffer zone between the two countries. Most importantly, the resolution ordered Iraq to get rid of its chemical, biological, and nuclear weapons programs. A special commission, called UNSCOM, was formed to make sure Iraq disarmed. On March 3, 1991, Iraqi leaders agreed to obey the U.N. resolutions.

Responding to U.S. encouragement, Shiites in southern Iraq revolted against Saddam in March. However, the Iraqi army had not been completely destroyed, and Saddam used it to brutally suppress the rebellion. The army then moved north, ruthlessly putting down a second revolt among the Kurds in April. Shiites and Kurds both felt betrayed by the United States, which had done nothing to help them. The United Nations condemned the attacks in Resolution 688, and in April coalition aircraft began patrolling a "no-fly zone" over northern Iraq to protect the Kurds. A second no-fly zone was established over southern Iraq in August 1992. The no-fly zones helped prevent further attacks by Saddam's forces on Kurds and Shiites.

Although the U.N. had given Iraq 105 days to disarm, the process took much longer. Iraqis tried to hamper UNSCOM efforts to find and destroy the prohibited weapons. They prevented inspectors from searching certain areas. When the inspectors discovered important documents related to the nuclear program, Iraqi officials tried to take them away. The Iraqis hid their biological weapons program for several years, until a high-ranking Iraqi official told UNSCOM how to find it.

Over the next several years, Iraq's attempts to obstruct UNSCOM led to additional U.N. resolutions condemning the country. To force Iraq to disarm, the U.N. maintained economic sanctions. These had little effect on Saddam Hussein but took a harsh toll on Iraqi citizens, who faced shortages of clean water, healthy food, and medical facilities. As people outside Iraq learned about the effect on civilians, they asked for sanctions to be lifted. Beginning in 1996, the U.N.'s "oil-for-food" program permitted Iraq to sell some of its oil and use the proceeds to purchase food and medicine. However, Saddam was able to divert a portion of the money raised for other uses.

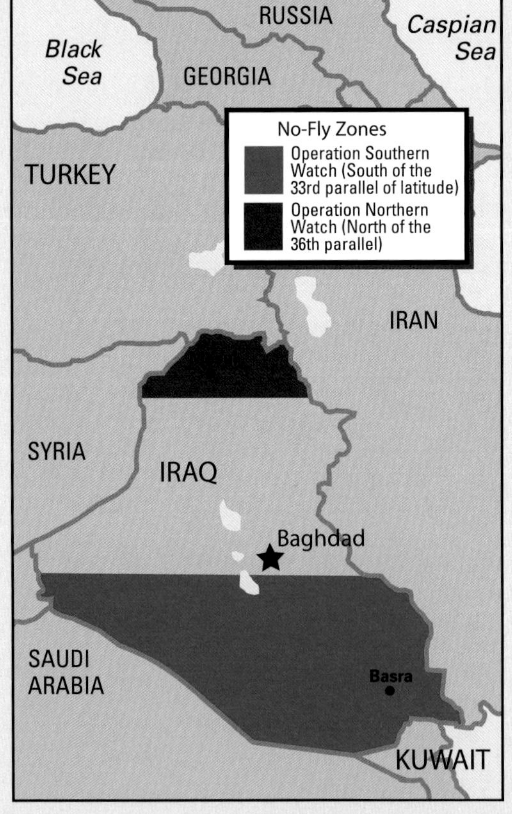

Because of Saddam's brutal repression of Shiite and Kurdish rebellions after the Gulf War, the United States and its coalition allies established "no-fly zones." These prevented Iraq from flying aircraft over the northern and southern areas of the country. U.S. and British fighter jets patrolled the no-fly zones to prevent Saddam's military from attacking.

Vehicles carrying UNSCOM inspectors are stopped by Iraqi guards at a checkpoint in Baghdad. Between 1992 and 1998, Iraqi officials tried to block the work of the U.N. weapons inspectors.

Between 1992 and 1997, UNSCOM inspectors effectively shut down Iraq's nuclear program and destroyed its chemical and biological arsenal. But inspectors still believed Iraq had some weapons of mass destruction. They wanted to search Saddam's royal palace complexes, which included thousands of buildings. Iraq refused.

American leaders were angry at Saddam's defiance, and the crisis soon escalated. In October 1998, President Bill Clinton signed the Iraqi Liberation Act. This legislation promised $97 million to Iraqi groups opposed to Saddam Hussein. In response, Saddam refused to cooperate with UNSCOM at all. The United States and Great Britain threatened military action. U.N. Secretary-General Kofi Annan

General Anthony C. Zinni (top) discusses Operation Desert Fox during a briefing at the Pentagon. The bombing campaign in December 1998 targeted sites in Iraq that U.S. intelligence agents suspected were being used to produce weapons in violation of U.N. resolutions. The aerial photo (right) shows the damage to a factory believed to be manufacturing parts for long-range missiles.

intervened, and Saddam agreed to let the inspections resume in November. However, when UNSCOM chief Richard Butler reported continued interference, the inspectors left Iraq again in December.

On December 16, 1998, the United States and Great Britain launched Operation Desert Fox, a four-day bombing campaign against Iraq. President Clinton explained that the campaign's purpose was to "degrade" Iraq's ability to produce weapons of mass destruction.

Though Operation Desert Fox was a military success—more than 75 sites in Iraq were destroyed—it was a political failure. When the air strikes ended, Saddam Hussein refused to let the U.N. inspectors back into Iraq.

Also, many nations were growing more concerned about the effect sanctions were having on the people of Iraq. In 1999, three of the five permanent members of the U.N. Security Council—France, Russia, and China—called for disbanding UNSCOM and lifting the sanctions. By year's end, a new monitoring organization—the U.N. Monitoring, Verification, and Inspection Commission (UNMOVIC)—had replaced UNSCOM. However, the sanctions remained in place, and for the next four years Saddam Hussein refused to allow U.N. inspections.

The Threat of WMD

Secretary of Defense Donald Rumsfeld (left) meets with President George W. Bush and Vice President Dick Cheney to discuss the "war on terrorism." U.S. leaders used the September 11 terrorist attack on the World Trade Center (bottom left) and Pentagon to justify a new policy of striking potential threats before they could menace the United States.

5

On January 20, 2001, George W. Bush became the 43rd president of the United States. The oldest son of former president George H. W. Bush, he brought into his administration several people who had served under his father and played key roles in the 1991 Gulf War. Dick Cheney was his vice president, and Colin Powell was appointed secretary of state.

For the first eight months of his term, Bush followed the

existing U.S. policy toward Iraq. This "containment" policy involved patrolling the no-fly zones to keep Saddam from moving his army, and working through the U.N. to maintain sanctions until Iraq disarmed.

Things changed radically on September 11, 2001, when Muslim terrorists flew hijacked airplanes into the World Trade Center in New York City and the Pentagon near Washington, D.C. More than 3,000 Americans were killed in the attacks. Bush quickly declared a "war on terrorism." He warned that the United States would pursue terrorist groups and would attack any country that helped terrorists.

Bush's first target was al-Qaeda, a shadowy organization responsible for the September 11 attacks. A renegade Saudi millionaire named Osama bin Laden had created the group in 1989. Bin Laden, a devout Muslim, became angry when coalition soldiers were stationed in Saudi Arabia during the 1990–91 Gulf crisis. After the war, he was offended by the continued presence of U.S. troops near Mecca, the holiest shrine in Islam. Soon, bin Laden and his followers were training terrorists and encouraging attacks against Western targets, hoping to drive the "infidel" soldiers out of the Middle East.

Since 1996, bin Laden and al-Qaeda had been based in Afghanistan. After the September 11

An FBI photo of Osama bin Laden, the al-Qaeda leader believed responsible for the September 11, 2001, attack on the United States. Although both bin Laden and Saddam Hussein opposed the United States, bin Laden refused to have anything to do with Saddam. In fact, the al-Qaeda leader considered Saddam an "enemy of Islam," and he encouraged Muslims to overthrow his regime.

attacks, the United States insisted that Afghanistan's Taliban government arrest and hand over the terrorist leader. When the Taliban refused, the United States and its allies invaded Afghanistan in October 2001. They soon overthrew the repressive Taliban, destroyed al-Qaeda's terrorist training camps, and forced bin Laden into hiding.

But even before the fighting in Afghanistan had started, U.S. leaders were thinking about Iraq. According to the *9/11 Commission Report*, immediately after the terrorist attacks occurred both President Bush and Defense Secretary Donald Rumsfeld had asked aides to find out whether Iraq was responsible. On September 15, during a meeting at the presidential retreat at Camp

David, Deputy Secretary of Defense Paul Wolfowitz argued that the United States should immediately attack Iraq, not Afghanistan. However, Wolfowitz could not prove a connection between Iraq and al-Qaeda, and Colin Powell convinced the president to focus on Afghanistan first.

Over the next few months, Bush's advisers debated ways to deal with potentially dangerous nations. The administration became divided into two camps. On one side were Powell and a few others who believed that working through the United Nations, using diplomacy and economic sanctions, was the best way to

U.S. Marines on patrol in an Afghan village. The 2001 invasion had broad international support: the United Nations condemned the September 11 terrorist attacks, and dozens of countries promised to assist the U.S. "war on terrorism."

contain potential threats. On the other side were Wolfowitz, Rumsfeld, Cheney, and others who proposed a new approach: the United States should strike at potential threats before it was attacked. Most experts in international law said this policy, known as "preemptive war," violated the U.N. charter, which prohibits countries from attacking each other, or using force except in self-defense. However, Cheney, Rumsfeld, and Wolfowitz argued that a preemptive war launched to prevent a future attack could be considered self-defense, rather than a war of aggression.

Eventually, Bush embraced the concept of preemptive war, which became the central element of a new U.S. foreign policy known as the Bush Doctrine. Another part of the Bush Doctrine was that the United States would work alone, if necessary, to protect its interests. In the past, U.S. leaders had sought help for military actions from traditional allies such as France, Germany, and Britain. According to the Bush Doctrine, the United States could attack any state posing a serious potential threat even if its allies did not support the use of force.

In early 2002, the Bush administration publicly identified Iran, North Korea, and Iraq as potential threats. U.S. intelligence agents believed all three countries were trying to develop nuclear weapons. All three had also assisted terrorists in the past, although none had been associated with al-Qaeda.

Although there had been no connection between Iraq and the September 11 attacks, the Bush administration decided that the logical next step in the "war on terrorism" was to remove Saddam Hussein from power. The Department of Defense began drafting plans for an invasion of Iraq. The government also began a public-relations campaign to convince the world that such an attack was justified. Administration officials said they had secret evidence proving the existence of Saddam Hussein's WMD programs. They discussed potential scenarios in which terrorists smuggled a nuclear bomb or chemical weapon built by Iraq into a U.S. city. In October 2002, Congress passed a resolution giving President Bush authority to "defend the national security of the United States against the continuing threat posed by Iraq."

U.S. diplomats pressured the United Nations to force Iraq to comply with the 16 relevant Security Council resolutions that had been passed since 1991. On September 12, 2002, President Bush told the U.N. General Assembly that Iraq had developed weapons of mass destruction. He recounted Saddam's history of violence against his own people, and he tried to link the regime to international terrorism. Bush

During 2002, both National Security Advisor Condoleeza Rice (left) and Central Intelligence Agency (CIA) director George Tenet stated publicly that Iraq possessed weapons of mass destruction.

implied that the United States was prepared to attack Iraq to enforce the U.N.'s resolutions—even if the U.N. itself did not support such an attack.

Iraq denied the charges. Iraqi leaders soon met in Vienna with Hans Blix, executive director of UNMOVIC, and Mohamed ElBaradei, director general of the International Atomic Energy Agency (IAEA). The Iraqis agreed to permit "unfettered" U.N. inspections to resume immediately.

After eight weeks of heated discussion, on November 8, 2002, the Security Council approved Resolution 1441. This resolution offered Iraq "a final opportunity to comply with its disarmament obligations." Saddam's regime was given 30 days to present a complete report on its WMD programs, and U.N. teams were to be given complete and immediate access to any site they wished to inspect.

On November 18, UNMOVIC and IAEA teams resumed inspections, and on December 7, Iraq submitted a 12,000-page report on its weapons programs. However, U.N. experts felt the report was incomplete. And as their work progressed, the inspectors made some disturbing discoveries. For example, an UNMOVIC team found 11 artillery shells that had not been mentioned in Iraq's December 7 report. The hollow shells could be used to carry chemical agents. Although Iraqi leaders said they had accidentally been overlooked, the inspectors were suspicious. Also, the inspectors found thousands of hidden documents related to weapons programs, which should have been turned over to the U.N. Finally, a number of Iraqi scientists refused to cooperate with inspectors. On January 27, 2003, Hans Blix told the Security Council, "Iraq appears not to have come to a genuine acceptance, not even today, of the disarmament which was demanded of it."

On February 5, 2003, Colin Powell spoke to the United Nations. He used U.S. intelligence reports—

several of which later turned out to be wrong—in an effort to prove that Saddam Hussein was still trying to fool the U.N. inspectors. He said that war was justified because of Iraq's WMD program, along with Saddam's human rights abuses and support of terrorism. He argued that the U.N. should support a war against Iraq. The Security Council was not convinced. France, Russia, China, and other nations insisted that Resolution 1441 did not automatically authorize war.

Despite this opposition, U.S. and British leaders began preparing for a military intervention in Iraq.

Colin Powell (inset) tells members of the U.N. Security Council that Iraq is hiding weapons of mass destruction, February 5, 2003.

They began to enlist other countries to join them in forcing Saddam Hussein from power. Spain, Japan, Australia, and South Korea offered support, as did dozens of smaller countries. Bush referred to these countries as the "coalition of the willing." However, some critics complained that the United States had essentially bribed these allies by offering financial incentives, trade agreements, or other valuable concessions in exchange for their support.

Most people outside of the United States—and many U.S. citizens as well—opposed war with Iraq.

Anti-war demonstrators kneel and pray near police barricades in front of the White House, March 19, 2003.

Protests and peace marches were held in New York, London, Paris, Tokyo, and other major cities. Crowds of angry Muslims burned American flags to protest U.S. policies in the Middle East. Critics of the Bush administration argued that Iraq was a diversion from the "war on terrorism." Many believed the United States simply wanted to seize control of the country's oil.

In February, the United States and Great Britain proposed a new resolution stating that Iraq had failed to meet its obligations under Resolution 1441. This would clear the way for war. France, Russia, China, Germany, and other countries opposed this new resolution. They wanted to let the U.N. inspectors continue their work. UNMOVIC and IAEA reports from February and early March had indicated that the inspectors were making progress, but that more time was needed. U.S. and British leaders believed Iraq had already been given enough time. Amid bitter disagreement, the draft resolution was withdrawn.

The United States and Britain claimed that because Iraq was a threat to their security, they did not need U.N. permission to remove Saddam. On March 17, 2003, Bush gave Saddam Hussein 48 hours to leave Iraq. When Saddam was still there on March 20, the coalition launched the Iraq War.

The
Occupation
of Iraq

By mid-April, U.S. and British forces had routed the Iraqi army, and statues of Saddam Hussein were being hauled down. The search for WMD in Iraq was not as successful as the initial military campaign, however. By January 2004, inspectors like Dr. David Kay (bottom left) concluded that U.S. intelligence reports had been wrong, and that Saddam had not possessed stockpiles of banned weapons.

6

In the first weeks of the 2003 Iraq War, U.S. tanks and infantry raced across the desert toward Baghdad, while British troops captured strategic cities and oil fields in southern Iraq. On April 9, U.S. troops entered Baghdad, forcing Saddam and his government to flee. Americans helped Iraqis pull down enormous statues of the dictator, to show that Saddam's power had ended. By May 1, President Bush declared the end of "major combat operations."

This did not mean peace had returned to Iraq. As Iraq's government collapsed, there was no longer an army or police force to preserve order in the cities. U.S. soldiers tried to protect electrical plants, water facilities, and oil pipelines, but there were not enough troops to prevent looting and violence. Priceless treasures were stolen from museums, and banks were robbed. Armed gangs roved city streets, making it unsafe for civilians to leave their homes.

Although many Iraqis were thankful to see Saddam gone, they resented the presence of coalition troops. Some began to wage an ***insurgency*** against the soldiers occupying the country. Resistance fighters launched surprise attacks against U.S. patrols. Homemade bombs were used to blow up security checkpoints, military convoys, and civilian targets. When U.S. soldiers arrested insurgents, more Iraqis became angry and joined the rebels.

As soon as Baghdad was captured, inspectors began looking for Iraq's weapons of mass destruction. The Iraq Survey Group (ISG), made up of U.S., British, and Australian experts, began to inspect hundreds of sites. Although before the war the CIA had reported that Iraq might have stockpiles of nuclear, biological, and chemical weapons, the inspectors did not find any useable weapons.

On September 30, 2004, the Iraq Survey Group released its final report. It said that Iraq had not produced weapons of mass destruction since 1991, and possessed no WMD when it was invaded in March 2003. However, the ISG report said that Saddam had tried to preserve the knowledge and equipment needed to make the banned weapons, so that he could restart the programs once U.N. economic sanctions were lifted.

A second justification for the war—the link with terrorism—also proved to be weak. After the war investigators confirmed that there had never been a direct relationship between Iraq and al-Qaeda. The *9/11 Commission Report*, released in July 2004, declared that Iraq had nothing to do with the September 11 attack. After the Iraq War ended, however, terrorists flocked to Iraq to join the insurgency, and al-Qaeda used anger among Muslims at the U.S. invasion to recruit new members. As a result, many experts concluded that the occupation in Iraq might ultimately increase the threat of global terrorism.

Although Bush and other U.S. leaders had been wrong about the threat that Iraq posed, they were tragically correct when they said that Saddam Hussein had cruelly mistreated the Iraqi people. After the war hundreds of mass graves were found, containing the bodies of more than 300,000 people murdered by the regime. Following Saddam's capture in December 2003, U.S. leaders promised to let the Iraqi people put the dictator on trial for crimes against humanity.

Saddam Hussein was an evil man, and most people agreed that Iraq, and the world, was better off without him in power. But the cost to remove him proved high. The Iraq War—and the ensuing insurgency—claimed the lives of at least 25,000 Iraqi citizens. (Some estimates place the number as high as 100,000.) Although fewer than 150 U.S. soldiers were killed during the war, over 10 times that many died in the two years that followed. And with each passing month, the death toll continued to mount. Meanwhile, the United States spent more than $200 billion on the war and occupation of Iraq.

There were other costs as well. Important resources that could have been used in the effort to destroy al-Qaeda and other terrorist groups were diverted to the mission in Iraq. In addition, by overstating the danger posed by Iraq, and by waging war without broad international support, the United States damaged the trust and goodwill of longtime allies.

The future of Iraq remains uncertain. In January 2005, millions of Iraqis went to the polls to vote in a historic election. Although this was a promising

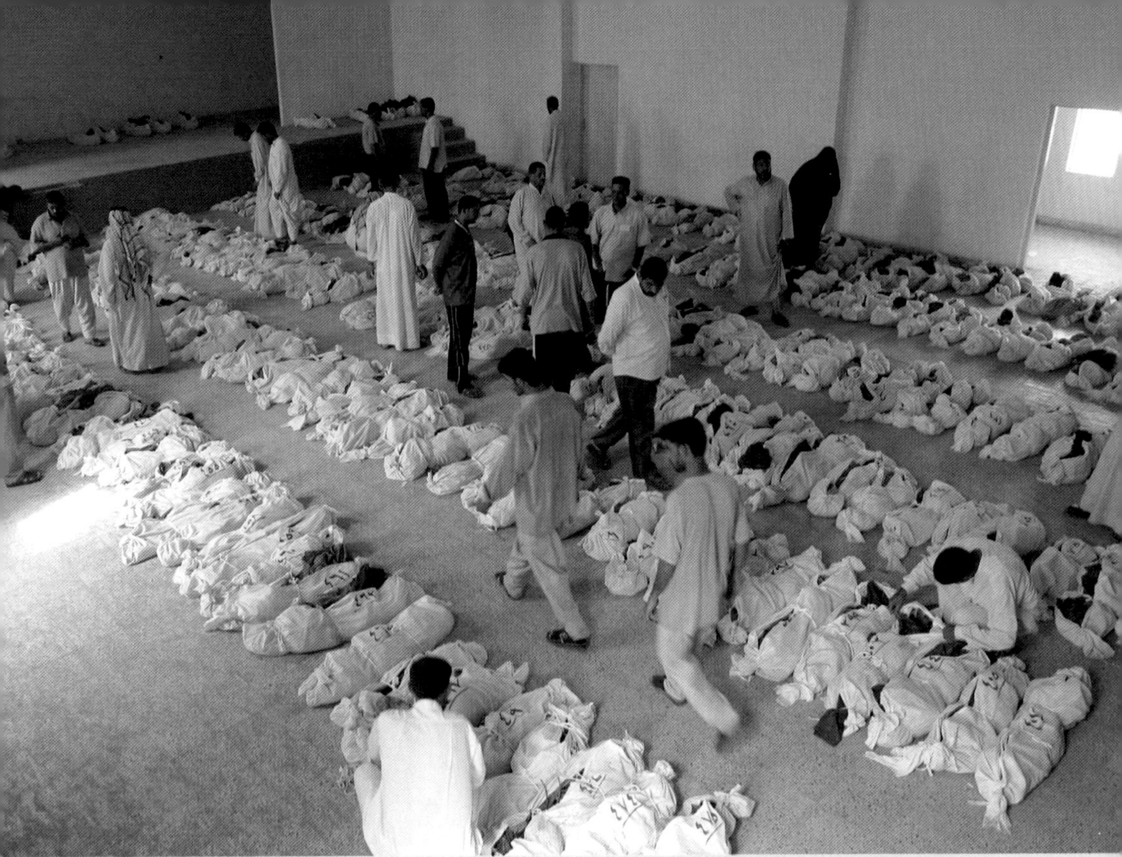

Iraqis search for relatives or friends among the remains of bodies found in a mass grave in Iraq.

development, Iraq's Sunnis, Shiites, and Kurds had great difficulty agreeing on the shape of their new government. Some experts worried that such disagreements might ultimately ignite a civil war. To prevent this, and to help the Iraqi government defeat the insurgency, it seems certain that the U.S. military will remain involved in Iraq for years to come.

Chronology

1979 Saddam Hussein becomes president of Iraq.

1980 Iraq invades Iran in September.

1987 Saddam Hussein begins the al-Anfal campaign against Iraqi Kurds, in which hundreds of thousands are killed or left homeless.

1988 A cease-fire ends the Iran-Iraq War; Iraq asks OPEC to increase its production quota.

1990 Tensions between Iraq and Kuwait rise, leading to Iraq's invasion on August 2. The United Nations condemns the attack. George H. W. Bush, the U.S. president, takes the lead in building a coalition of nations opposed to Iraq's aggression. On November 29, the U.N. Security Council passes Resolution 678, which threatens military action if Iraq does not withdraw from Kuwait by January 15.

1991 The Gulf War begins on January 17 with a bombing campaign. After six weeks, a ground campaign begins. The Iraqi army is routed in 100 hours, and a cease-fire is declared. Saddam agrees to comply with U.N. resolutions requiring him to disarm. The coalition establishes a no-fly zone over northern Iraq to protect the Kurds from Saddam's forces.

1992 A second no-fly zone is established over the southern part of Iraq, to protect Shiites.

1995 An Iraqi defector tells UNSCOM inspectors about Saddam's secret biological weapons program. The program is subsequently destroyed.

1997 Iraq refuses to allow UNSCOM to inspect Saddam's palaces. Scott Ritter, an American member of UNSCOM, is accused of being a spy and expelled from Iraq.

1998 The crisis over inspections culminates in Operation Desert Fox, a four-day bombing campaign.

2001 George W. Bush is inaugurated as president of the United States. On September 11, terrorists attack the World Trade Center and Pentagon. In response, the U.S. launches its "war on terrorism" and attacks Afghanistan.

2002 The Bush Doctrine declares that the United States will use preemptive war when necessary to protect its interests. U.S. leaders urge the United Nations to force Iraq to comply with U.N. resolutions, and Bush administration officials begin planning for war. In November, the U.N. Security Council passes Resolution 1441, which offers Iraq a "final opportunity" to disarm. Saddam agrees to allow inspections to resume.

2003 Despite pressure from the United Nations, the United States, Britain, and their allies launch a war against Iraq on March 20. On April 9, Saddam and his government are forced to leave Baghdad as U.S. troops occupy the city. In December, Saddam is found hiding on a small farm and is captured.

2004 On June 28, the coalition hands over power to an interim Iraqi government, although U.S. and British forces remain in the country. On July 22, the *9/11 Commission Report* confirms that there had been no link between Iraq and al-Qaeda. On September 30, the Iraq Survey Group reports that Saddam did not possess weapons of mass destruction at the time Iraq was invaded.

2005 In January, Iraqis go to the polls to elect a new government. U.S. troops remain in Iraq, battling a violent insurgency.

Glossary

AUTONOMOUS—politically independent and self-governing.

COALITION—a temporary union between multiple countries to achieve a common goal.

COLONIALISM—a policy in which one country directly rules outlying territories and uses their labor and resources to increase its power.

CREDITOR—a country or person owed money by another.

ECONOMIC SANCTIONS—restrictions imposed to punish a country by preventing it from purchasing (or selling) goods and services.

GLUT—a larger supply of something than is needed.

INSURGENCY—a rebellion or uprising against a government.

MANDATE—the authority, granted by the League of Nations to an established power like Great Britain or France, to administer a less developed territory. Under the mandate system, the more established countries were expected to help the new nations develop good governments and the social institutions required for stability and independence.

NATIONALISM—the desire by a people who share a language and culture to gain a politically independent state of their own.

PROTECTORATE—a country that is defended and controlled by a more powerful state.

RESOLUTION—a formal expression of a decision by the United Nations Security Council, considered binding under international law.

STALEMATE—a situation in which neither of two opposing sides can win.

TRIBUTE—a payment made by one country to another, as a sign of submission.

WEAPONS OF MASS DESTRUCTION (WMD)—weapons, such as biological or chemical agents or nuclear warheads, that are capable of killing large numbers of people.

Further Reading

Books for Students:

Carlisle, Rodney P. *Iraq War*. New York: Facts On File, 2005.

———. *Persian Gulf War*. New York: Facts On File, 2003.

Downing, David. *Iraq: 1968–2003*. Chicago: Raintree, 2004.

Stewart, Gail. *Saddam Hussein*. San Diego: Lucent Books, 2005.

Thompson, Bill. *Iraq*. Philadelphia: Mason Crest Publishers, 2004.

Books for Older Readers:

Atkinson, Rick. *Crusade: The Untold Story of the Persian Gulf War.* New York: Houghton Mifflin, 1993.

David, Peter. *Triumph in the Desert: The Challenge, the Fighting, the Legacy.* New York: Random House, 1991.

Keegan, John. *The Iraq War*. New York: Knopf, 2004.

Murray, Williamson, and Robert H. Scales, Jr. *The Iraq War: A Military History.* New York: Belknap Press, 2003.

The 9/11 Commission Report: Final Report of the National Commission on Terrorist Attacks upon the United States. New York: W. W. Norton, 2004.

Sifry, Micah L., and Christopher Cerf. *The Iraq War Reader: History, Documents, Opinions.* New York: Touchstone, 2003.

Internet Resources

http://www.state.gov/p/nea/rls/01fs/14906.htm

This website of the U.S. State Department includes links to each of the U.N. Security Council resolutions on Iraq from 1990 to 2002.

http://www.cnn.com/SPECIALS/2001/gulf.war/index.html

Web page for the 2001 CNN special "The Unfinished War: A Decade Since Desert Storm," which contains articles about the UNSCOM inspections, the effect of U.N. sanctions, and Operation Desert Fox, among other subjects.

http://www.pbs.org/wgbh/pages/frontline/gulf/

This site is a companion to the *Frontline* program "The Gulf War," with links to oral accounts from both decision-makers and ordinary soldiers, information about the 1990–91 Gulf crisis, and a detailed chronology.

http://www.cnn.com/SPECIALS/2003/iraq/

A comprehensive Web page with reports and information about the 2003 Iraq War.

http://www.defendamerica.gov/

The official U.S. government website about the "war on terrorism" includes current news about the continuing occupation of Afghanistan and Iraq.

http://www.cia.gov/cia/reports/iraq_wmd_2004/

The text of a 2004 CIA report, which found that Iraq did not possess weapons of mass destruction at the time the United States invaded in 2003.

http://www.un.org/News/

This website of the United Nations includes links to articles about current U.N. programs in Iraq.

Publisher's Note: The websites listed on this page were active at the time of publication. The publisher is not responsible for websites that have changed their address or discontinued operation since the date of publication.

Numbers in ***bold italics*** refer to captions.

Picture Credits

Page:
2: U.S. Department of Defense
7: U.S. Department of State; U.S. Department of Defense; U.S. Department of Defense
8: Reuters/Corbis
12: Michael Spencer/Saudi Aramco World/PADIA
16-17: © OTTN Publishing
19: © OTTN Publishing
22: Corel Corporation
24: INA/AFP/Getty Images
24-25: William Foley/Time Life Pictures/Getty Images
27: Hulton Archive/Getty Images
29: IRNA/AFP/Getty Images
32: U.S. Department of Defense
34: Mona Sharaf/AFP/Getty Images
36: George Bush Presidential Library
36-37: U.S. Department of Defense
39: U.S. Department of Defense
40: U.S. Department of Defense
41: U.S. Department of Defense
42: U.S. Department of Defense
44: © OTTN Publishing
45: Scott Peterson/Liaison/Getty Images
46: U.S. Department of Defense
48: Peter C. Brandt/Getty Images
48-49: U.S. Department of Defense
51: Federal Bureau of Investigation
52: U.S. Department of Defense
55: U.S. State Department; Central Intelligence Agency
57: Mario Tama/Getty Images; (inset) U.S. State Department
58: Mike Theiler/Getty Images
60: Stephen Jaffe/AFP/Getty Images
60-61: Mirrorpix/Getty Images
65: Thomas Hartwell/USAID

Front Cover: Patrick De Noirmont/Reuters/Landov (top); Peter Jordan/Time Life Pictures/Getty Images (inset)
Back Cover: U.S. Department of Defense

About the Author

Jim Gallagher is the author of more than 20 books for young readers, including *The Johnstown Flood* and *Ferdinand Magellan and the First Voyage Around the World*. He lives in New Jersey with his wife, LaNelle, and their son, Donald.